TITUS AND PHILEMON

by
Deb Fennema

FAITH
ALIVE®
Christian Resources

Grand Rapids, Michigan

Cover photo: PhotoDisc Green

Faith Alive Christian Resources published by CRC Publications.
Discover Your Bible series. *Discover Titus and Philemon* (Study Guide), © 2003 by CRC Publications, 2850 Kalamazoo Ave. SE, Grand Rapids, MI 49560.

We welcome your comments. Call us at 1-800-333-8300 or e-mail us at editors@faithaliveresources.org.

ISBN 1-59255-180-7

10 9 8 7 6 5 4 3 2 1

Contents

How to Study

The questions in this study booklet will help you discover for yourself what the Bible says. This is inductive Bible study—no one will tell you what the Bible says or what to believe. You will discover the message for yourself.

Questions are the key to inductive Bible study. Through questions you will search for the writers' thoughts and ideas. The prepared questions in this booklet are designed to help you in your quest for answers. You can and should ask your own questions too. The Bible comes alive with meaning for many people as they discover for themselves the exciting truths it contains. Our hope and prayer is that this booklet will help the Bible come alive for you.

The questions in this study are designed to be used with the New International Version of the Bible, but other translations can also be used.

Step 1. Read each Bible passage several times. Allow the thoughts and ideas to sink in. Think about its meaning. Ask questions of your own about the passage.

Step 2. Answer the questions, drawing your answers from the passage. Remember that the purpose of the study is to discover what the Bible says. Write your answers in your own words. If you use Bible study aids such as commentaries or Bible handbooks, do so only after completing your own personal study.

Step 3. Apply the Bible's message to your own life and world. Ask yourself these questions: What is this passage saying to me? How does it challenge me? Comfort me? Encourage me? Is there a promise I should claim? A warning I should heed? For what can I give thanks? If you sense God speaking to you in some way, respond to God in a personal prayer.

Step 4. Share your thoughts with someone else if possible. This will be easiest if you are part of a Bible study group that meets regularly to share discoveries and discuss questions. If you would like to learn of a study group in your area or if you would like more information on how to start a small group Bible study,

- write to Discover Your Bible at

2850 Kalamazoo Ave. SE	or	P.O. Box 5070
Grand Rapids, MI 49560		STN LCD 1
		Burlington, ON L7R 3Y8

- call toll-free 1-888-644-0814, e-mail *smallgroups@crcna.org*, or visit *www.SmallGroupMinistries.org* (for training advice and general information)

- call toll-free 1-800-333-8300 or visit *www.FaithAliveResources.org* (to order materials)

Introduction

The apostle Paul wrote many letters—to individuals as well as churches—and several of those letters are preserved in the Bible. In this study we'll be looking closely at two of them, now commonly known as the New Testament books of Titus and Philemon.

Titus, a young man whom Paul had met in the early years of his ministry, had become a fellow worker and faithful companion on Paul's missionary journeys, and Philemon, a well-to-do householder whom Paul had met later (probably near Colosse), had become a faithful, generous supporter of Paul's ministry and had opened his home so that other believers could worship there. Paul considered each of these men a close friend.

While the brief letters Paul wrote to Titus and Philemon are addressed to them individually, it's clear that these letters are also intended for the groups of believers (churches) who worshiped and associated with them. In both letters Paul speaks of godly living, but in each he gives a different emphasis. In the letter to Titus we find important instructions about principles for Christian living, and in the letter to Philemon we find Paul applying Christian principles to a specific situation.

Studying Titus and Philemon in sequence proves interesting. In the letter to Titus we learn from Paul's direct manner as he faces a challenge head-on—dealing with false teachers and unchristian behavior on the island of Crete. And in the letter to Philemon we learn from Paul's diplomacy and tact as he handles a delicate situation with great care—urging a fellow Christian to receive back a runaway slave as a Christian brother. In both letters we see how important it is to share the good news of Jesus and to live faithfully for Christ as people of integrity.

Glossary of Terms

Apollos—a pastor from Alexandria who had been taught by Paul's friends Priscilla and Aquila and had become well known as an effective preacher of the gospel (Acts 18:26-28; 1 Cor. 3:4-6; Titus 3:13).

Apphia—one of the persons addressed in Paul's letter to Philemon. She is probably Philemon's wife.

apostle—a person sent by God to accomplish a special task.

Aristarchus—a fellow worker with Paul, this person is also described as Paul's fellow prisoner in Paul's letter to the Colossians. Aristarchus, Demas, Epaphras, Luke, and Mark are all mentioned in the closing comments of Paul's letters to Philemon and to the Colossians; scholars agree that both of these letters were likely written and delivered at the same time (see Col. 4:7-17; Philem. 2, 10, 23-24).

Archippus—another of the persons addressed in Paul's letter to Philemon (see also Col. 4:17). Archippus may have been Philemon's son or another close relative. He was apparently a member of Philemon's household and of the church that met in Philemon's home.

Artemas—one of the persons mentioned near the end of Paul's letter to Titus. Paul said he would send either Artemas or Tychicus to Titus, apparently to continue Titus's work in Crete so that Titus could visit Paul for a while or work elsewhere.

circumcision group—This term refers to a group of people who taught that a person had to become Jewish or had to hold to certain Jewish practices to be a Christian.

Crete, Cretans—Crete is the fourth largest island in the Mediterranean Sea. Its inhabitants were called Cretans.

Dalmatia—a region to the northwest of Greece in the days of the Roman Empire.

Demas—one of Paul's fellow workers (see **Aristarchus**).

elect—People who are elect have been chosen by God to have eternal life through Jesus Christ. This salvation is for all who believe in Jesus as the only Savior from sin and death. Anyone who trusts in Jesus as Savior and Lord is elect.

envy—Envy is a deeply malicious form of greed. It involves not just wanting something that you can't have but also wanting another person, viewed as a rival, not to have it either.

Epaphras—a fellow worker and prisoner with Paul (see **Aristarchus**).

faith—"being sure of what we hope for and certain of what we do not see" (Heb. 11:1). True faith involves the knowledge and assurance that God's Word in the Bible is trustworthy and true, giving us the confidence that all our sins are forgiven through the saving work of Christ.

foolish—In the Bible, being foolish means going against God, deciding not to follow God's way (see Ps. 14:1-3).

Gentiles—all people who are not Jews.

godliness—A person shows godliness by striving to live God's way, aiming to live a life pleasing to God.

grace—Often a greeting in Paul's letters, *grace* refers to God's unmerited favor, by which we can have eternal life through the saving work of Christ.

holy—pure, set apart in a special way to bring glory to God.

hope—In the Bible *hope* refers to a sure thing: the eternal life God promises for all who believe in Jesus for salvation (Rom. 1:16; Titus 1:2; Heb. 11:1). This is far different from a common meaning of *hope* that points toward wishing for something.

Jews—descendants of Abraham, God's chosen Old Testament people (also called Israelites or Hebrews).

justified—A person who is justified is a person who has been made right with God (righteous).

Luke—a friend and fellow worker with Paul. Luke is described as a doctor in Colossians 4:14 and is probably the same person who wrote the New Testament gospel of Luke and the book of Acts (see also **Aristarchus**).

Mark—may have been John Mark, who traveled and worked with Paul at different times and was probably the author of the New Testament gospel of Mark (see also **Aristarchus**).

Nicopolis—Several cities in the Roman Empire had this name, meaning "victory city," and the one mentioned in Titus was probably the metropolis on the northwestern shore of Greece.

peace—In the Bible peace is closely related to the Hebrew word *shalom*, which means well-being in line with God's will in every aspect of life.

righteous—A person who is righteous is right with God, having no guilt or sin. God grants us the righteousness of Christ when we believe in him as Savior and Lord.

saints—All who believe in Christ as Savior are *saints*, meaning those who are "set apart." Believers are set apart to live holy lives by faith in Christ—not in separation from the world but by being like Jesus, who associated with all kinds of people but did not join in their sin.

slanderers—people who practice malicious gossip, usually meant to damage the reputations of others for some sort of gain, such as power, prestige, status, or wealth.

Timothy—This fellow worker with the apostle Paul is mentioned at the beginning of several of Paul's letters in the New Testament. The Bible also includes two letters Paul wrote to this faithful Christian brother—now known as the books of 1 and 2 Timothy.

Tychicus—another of Paul's faithful, fellow workers in ministry (see also **Artemas**). Tychicus sometimes also carried news about Paul and letters from Paul to various churches (Col. 4:7-9).

Zenas—Zenas was a lawyer who apparently traveled with Apollos the preacher, as Paul mentions in his closing remarks to Titus. Zenas's Greek name suggests that he may have been a lawyer in the civil system.

Lesson 1

Titus 1

A Job for Titus

Introductory Notes

In Titus 1 we find important instructions that point to the beginnings of church government. No deacons are mentioned (as in Phil. 1:1; 1 Tim. 3:8-13), and it seems that elders were not yet firmly in place in the churches on the island of Crete. So in this letter, written around A.D. 64 in the early days of the church, Paul lays out some guidelines for Titus to use as he ministers to the churches of Crete.

1. *Titus 1:1-3*

    a. What do we learn about Paul from these verses?

    b. How are faith and knowledge described?

    c. How does God bring about faith and knowledge in people's lives?

2. *Titus 1:4*

    a. How does Paul describe Titus?

b.   What is the blessing Paul conveys on Titus?

3.   *Titus 1:5-9*

Why had Paul left Titus in Crete?

4.   *Titus 1:6-9*

What are the qualifications of an elder?

5.   *Titus 1:10-14*

a.   How does Paul describe the "rebellious people" in the churches of Crete?

b.   Note the way Paul says a Cretan had described his own people. Why do you think someone would say that?

c.   Why is it important that these Cretans be rebuked?

6. *Titus 1:15-16*

    a.   What do you think Paul means when he says nothing is pure to those who are corrupted and do not believe?

    b.   How can we tell whether a person knows God?

Questions for Reflection

What have you learned about "the trustworthy message" of salvation? In what ways can you share it with others?

In what ways can Paul's teachings about trustworthy church leaders help you serve God faithfully?

What can you tell others about the importance of sound teachings and the destructiveness of false teachings in the church?

Lesson 2

Titus 2

Living Godly Lives

Introductory Notes

Paul has made it clear that Titus should "straighten out" or put in order "what was left unfinished" of the church planting work in Crete (Titus 1:5). In Titus 2 we find there was a lot of work to do in teaching the people of Crete to live godly lives. And undergirding all this teaching was the example of "our God and Savior, Jesus Christ, who gave himself for us to redeem us from all wickedness and to purify for himself a people that are his very own, eager to do what is good" (2:13-14).

1. *Titus 2:1-2*

    a. By what standard was Titus to teach? Why?

    b. What was Titus to teach older men?

2. *Titus 2:3*

    What was Titus to teach older women?

3. *Titus 2:4-5*

    What were the older women to train younger women to do?

4. *Titus 2:6-8*

   a.   What was Titus to encourage in younger men?

   b.   What is Paul teaching here about personal integrity?

5. *Titus 2:9-10*

   a.   What was Titus to teach people who were slaves?

   b.   What was the purpose of these instructions?

6. *Titus 2:11-14*

   a.   What does God's grace teach?

   b.   For what are Paul, Titus, and all other believers waiting?

   c.   How are Jesus and his followers described?

7. **Titus 2:15**

   Why might Paul include the instructions in verse 15?

Questions for Reflection

   Have you ever been disillusioned about Christianity by observing the behavior of someone who claimed to be a Christian?

   In what ways have you been attracted to Christianity because of the behavior of someone who claimed to be a Christian?

Lesson 3

Titus 3

Doing Good for Jesus' Sake

Introductory Notes

In Titus 3 the apostle Paul again gives strongly worded admonitions to the church members of Crete. He begins by describing their relationship with civil government, which often became an issue for new believers because they began to profess Jesus as Lord rather than the Roman Caesar as Lord. Paul also describes the situation of being an unbeliever and how God brings salvation. Paul additionally cautions the people not to get caught up in meaningless discussions that are aimed at dividing the church. Then he closes his letter, as he often does, with warm greetings and personal notes.

1. *Titus 3:1-2*

   What instructions does Paul give for living in society?

2. *Titus 3:3-7*

   a. How does Paul describe the past that all believers have in common?

   b. Why did God save people? How?

   c. What do people become through God's salvation?

3. *Titus 3:8*

   Why does Paul want these teachings emphasized?

4. *Titus 3:9-11*

   a. What kinds of controversies does Paul describe?

   b. How was Titus to handle a divisive person? Why?

5. *Titus 3:12-15*

   a. In closing, what instructions does Paul give to Titus?

   b. What does Paul want the people to learn?

Questions for Reflection

   Are there any civil laws you find difficult to obey? If so, which ones?

Can you make a brief, convincing statement of your faith in Christ? Think about how you would share it with someone.

What good things do you (or could you) do in thankfulness for God's salvation?

Lesson 4
Philemon

Doing What Is Right, with Love

Introductory Notes

In Paul's letter to Philemon, written around A.D. 60, we find the apostle pleading with a friend to accept another person back into his household. That person, Onesimus, appears to have been a runaway slave, and Paul appeals to Philemon "on the basis of love" to accept this man back "no longer as a slave, but . . . as a brother in the Lord" (Philem. 9, 16). In this way we see Paul putting Christian principles into practice by chipping away at the wrongful institution of slavery, in the name of the Lord Jesus.

1. *Philemon 1-3*

   a. How are the writers of this letter described?

   b. How are the recipients of this letter described?

2. *Philemon 4-7*

   a. Describe Paul's prayer for Philemon.

   b. What has Philemon done for Paul? For other believers?

3. *Philemon 8-11*

    a. On what basis is Paul appealing to Philemon on behalf of Onesimus?

    b. How does Paul describe his relationship with Onesimus?

4. *Philemon 12-16*

    a. Why would Paul have liked to keep Onesimus with him?

    b. Why did Paul want Philemon's consent?

    c. How had Onesimus's situation changed while he was with Paul?

    d. What does Paul say about the reason for Onesimus's escape?

5. *Philemon 17-21*

    a.   Why should Philemon welcome Onesimus?

    b.   How does Paul offer to right "any wrong" that Onesimus might have done?

    c.   Do you think Philemon will do as Paul requests?

6. *Philemon 22-25*

Why might Paul return to Philemon?

Questions for Reflection

How do you think this story ends? Do you think Philemon frees Onesimus and perhaps even sends him back to help Paul in his ministry? Why or why not?

Think of a time in your (or someone else's) life when God brought a good result out of a bad situation. What happened?

In what ways does this letter to Philemon show how believers can apply various principles taught in the letter to Titus?

An Invitation

Listen now to what God is saying to you.

You may be aware of things in your life that keep you from coming near to God. You may have thought of God as unsympathetic, angry, and punishing. You may feel as if you don't know how to pray or how to come near to God.

"But because of his great love for us, God, who is rich in mercy, made us alive with Christ even when we were dead in transgressions—it is by grace you have been saved" (Eph. 2:4). Jesus, God's Son, died on the cross to save us from our sins. It doesn't matter where you come from, what you've done in the past, or what your heritage is. None of these things makes any difference to God. God has been watching over you and caring for you, drawing you closer. "And you also were included in Christ when you heard the word of truth, the gospel of your salvation" (Eph. 1:13).

So now do you want to receive Jesus as your Savior and Lord? It's as simple as A-B-C:

- **A**dmit that you have sinned and that you need God's forgiveness.
- **B**elieve that God loves you and that Jesus already paid the price for your sins.
- **C**ommit your life to God in prayer, asking God to forgive your sins, nurture you as his child, and fill you with the Holy Spirit.

Prayer of Commitment

Here is a prayer of commitment to Jesus Christ as Savior. If you long to be in a loving relationship with Jesus, pray this prayer. If you have already committed your life to Jesus, use this prayer for renewal and praise.

Dear God, I come to you simply and honestly to confess that I have sinned, that sin is a part of who I am. And yet I know that you listen to sinners who are truthful before you. So I come with empty hands and heart, asking for forgiveness.

I confess that only through faith in Jesus Christ can I come to you. I confess my need for a Savior, and I thank you, Jesus, for dying on the cross to pay the price for my sins. Lord, I ask that you forgive my sins and count me among those who are righteous in your sight. Remove the guilt that accompanies sin and bring me into your presence.

Holy Spirit of God, help me to pray, and teach me to live by your Word. Faithful God, help me to serve you faithfully. Make me more and more like Jesus each day, and help me to share with others the good news of your great salvation. In Jesus' name, Amen.

Recommended Reading

Barker, Kenneth L., et al. *The NIV Study Bible.* Grand Rapids, Mich.: Zondervan, 1985.

Barton, Bruce B. et al. *Life Application Bible Commentary: First and Second Timothy, Titus.* Carol Stream, Ill.: Tyndale, 1993.

Liefeld, Walter L. *The NIV Application Commentary: 1 and 2 Timothy, Titus.* Grand Rapids, Mich.: Zondervan, 1999.

"Slavery, Serfdom, and Forced Labor." *Encyclopedia Brittanica, 15th ed.* Chicago, London, et al.: Encyclopedia Britannica, Inc., 1981. 16:853-866.

Evaluation Questionnaire

DISCOVER TITUS AND PHILEMON

As you complete this study, please fill out this questionnaire to help us evaluate the effectiveness of our materials. Please be candid. Thank you.

1. Was this a home group ___ or a church-based ___ program? What church?

2. Was the study used for
   ___ a community evangelism group?
   ___ a community grow group?
   ___ a church Bible study group?

3. How would you rate the materials?

   Study Guide
   ___ excellent ___ very good ___ good ___ fair ___ poor

   Leader Guide
   ___ excellent ___ very good ___ good ___ fair ___ poor

4. What were the strengths?

5. What were the weaknesses?

6. What would you suggest to improve the material?

7. In general, what was the experience of your group?

Your name (optional)_____

Address _____

_____

8. Other comments:

(Please fold, tape, stamp, and mail. Thank you.)

Faith Alive Christian Resources
2850 Kalamazoo Ave. SE
Grand Rapids, MI 49560